Our Ship

Also by John Mole

The Love Horse
A Partial Light

Our Ship

John Mole

Secker & Warburg · London

First published in England 1977 by
Martin Secker & Warburg Limited
14 Carlisle Street, London W1V 6NN

Copyright © John Mole 1977

Designed by Philip Mann

436 28450 2

Printed in Great Britain by
Redwood Burn Limited
Trowbridge & Esher

To Simon and Ben

Acknowledgments

Poems in this collection have first appeared in *Ambit, The Cornhill Magazine, Encounter, The Listener, Meridian, The New Statesman, The New Review, PEN New Poems 1975, PEN New Poems 1976, Phoenix, Poetry Nation, Samphire, The Times Literary Supplement, Use of English, Workshop New Poetry.*

Pantomime Cat and **The Cenotaph at Coleorton** have appeared in limited editions from The Mandeville Press. **Landscapes** has been published previously as a pamphlet from The Priapus Press.

Contents

3

The Toy Piano

The mouth of the toy piano
grits its teeth. It bites
habitually on mice and teddy-bears
but is dissatisfied.

The wired belly tinkles
for stronger meat,
those harmonies of suffering
beyond the cradle.

Branches of dark forests
where each bird has earned its song
enchant the piano.
Only what hurts matters

and this child will matter
when he is not a child.
But while they play together
in a lighted room

the piano hates him.

From the West

Sent from the west
where fashions die more slowly
and the sun comes down —
We write "This place
is perfect. Who

could ever be unhappy here?"
A short walk
out to the shops, exact
provisions parcelled up —
a loaf, brown eggs.

The light goes gently
on these soft horizons;
all the books we brought
we have not read.
Words, words ...

Four bright squares
of landscape and a postmark
speak for us;
our only messages
are Greetings

from the yachts, the picnics,
ponies nuzzling our children's
sugared hands, and from
a central silence
in the empty blue.

Yachts

Flattened against the air,
a distant passage of skilled
triangles like words withheld —

No awkwardness of management.
Beyond our reach, their silent
balance is articulate

as if we might
lie down forever here
and gently follow them from sight.

LANDSCAPES
"A man sees nothing in nature but what he knows"

John Constable

1

Caught without paints
beside the fall at Terni —
what was there left to say but
"Well done, water, by God!" ?

Another's chartered brush
was too much with him:
"We must jog on and be content ...
I'm sick of portraits."

Lucky the third
who called out "Hawkey!
Look at this thunder-storm —
Oh isn't it sublime?"

2   The Cenotaph at Coleorton

A noble stag
made Landseer's fortune,
groomed, upholstered
on its décor peak.

"Behold" it cried
in fustian Shakespeare
"I am Nature
tipped with gilt."

But here the antlered
trees reduce
a stag's rococo
to some lesser branch

and wisps of cloud
are temperate
where wealthy salons
cultivate the wild.

3   Mr and Mrs Robert Andrews

The repose of their moon-faces,
a complete languor —
his sporting deshabille,
her silk confection
set insouciantly there
as if the landscape
sought its definition
in their limpid gaze

but failed, as if
it might define them
if they turned their heads
less proudly from us now
to see those clouds above
a fragile harvest
and the world encroaching
on each fold of blue.

4

Sold for a round harmony
of golden guineas!
Jingle jingle went the coins
in Ruskin's pocket.

He knew what he knew —
A moral aesthete
hungry for sublimities —
The Revolution water-marked by Taste.

Imagination, cloaked
in Lakeland grandeur, sweeping
publicly a genius
from *Modern Painters* —

"Which part of the picture
is the bridge?" Despite so much,
the laughter in that court
resounds against him.

5

Her husband takes the photographs
from every angle with his special lens.
All nature in obedient arrest
corrects a raindrop wobbling on its leaf.

O glacé universe! "My paintings sell.
I keep them down to five by three.
A gallery somewhere is doing prints."
The public needs unlimited editions.

On display, those spectral horses
leap from their waves beneath the moon
but something quiet above the fireplace —
Landscape mellowed by electric coals.

Three Loves

Immediate love given
retrieves no light
from the dark places;
its touch is too sudden
and without weight.

Love held back
between delicate faces
is darker still;
too much time passes
in each shy smile.

Only love intent
as light on the sea
finds a trick
which dazzles, the accident
of You and Me.

Con Amore

She practises the clarinet,
her back turned to a spacious window.

No sound reaches the garden.
Music, on a stalk of silence,

waves behind glass.
She turns her own pages.

Phrase by phrase
the theme is movement only

as the flowers all know
inclined towards her.

Love must blossom on its stalk
before she hears it,

and the pages turn
like a white rose opening.

FROM AN AUTUMN NOTEBOOK

Late Romantic

Hollyhocks, our
pair of them —
pure Tennyson.

It takes more
than a garden fence
to blast romance —

In verse they
hang heavily,
here they hang heavily

with dust on three
closed blooms,
their leaves skeletons.

October Mornings

1
always spared me
this before —

a cold sun
heavy with sentence

exacted always
less than this before —

the bright leaves
gagged on their branches,

a language
rooted in dusk,

no poems
not even this one

2
but at first light
it is his need I wake to,

the necessary small-talk
in another room —

it will be late soon enough
without our aid

and how did we lease
the terms we speak on?

Child, we have planted you
here in our place —

seedling, purpose
of what is left to say.

Little Storms

bother at glass.
Their wet batters.

Hollows of the garden
darkly collect them

and two bottles
on the doorstep, milky

filling with a pale
clouded dilution.

It takes dry hours
to carry them off

or the small clink
of our regular order.

Treasure Island

He put to sea
in a silver galleon,
the brooch that glittered
on his mother's breast.

Each night she folded his clothes
and kissed him;
a clean shirt thirsted
for the quenching moon.

Such lost heroics,
pinned to the mast-head
by a pirate's knife,
the warm blood coming

coming and going
and gone forever —
The moon reminds him
when he cannot sleep.

Looking at Daffodils, in the Old Fashion

Their fierce display was current briefly:
Crisp on its stalk, each golden horn
Is paper-money now. What reason
For such innocent and natural treason?
Who bought whom? To be unborn
And not betrayed to death! But chiefly

This: that what is left may buy
Something back still from so much taken —
Neither to haggle at the price
Nor wait for sensible, informed advice
But *now*. Before the last is shaken
Earthwards. Not to know how, yet try.

The First of Summer

Even the old must tackle this.
They push each other in their chairs.

The young in one another's arms
read *Notes on Shakespeare*.

Ice-cream bells play Colonel Bogey.
Someone says "When I was your age ..."

Mottled faces, patterned rugs,
O scented cotton sprinkled with desire!

Our Ship

At last, on that cold bright day,
Our ship reached home.
There had been a delay.

I boarded it alone,
Remember? Though I knew
You wanted to come.

And afterwards, when I told you
There was nothing — all lost,
No comfits, no crew —

I lied. At what cost
We soon discovered,
But that's in the past.

The truth, then? A small bird
Dead on the cabin floor;
As I watched, its wings stirred

Very gently. Nothing more,
I promise, that was all —
Except that I saw

A packet on the table
Marked with your name, and took
And kept it from you out of fear

And here it is. And look,
I still don't know
What's in it. Take it now.

"I Say We Shall Have No More Marriages"

I brought the daggers from the place —
Unwise, perhaps, but still
we learned, on coming face to face,
that looks can also kill.

The days pass tediously now,
the stones can't hear our tread,
and when night falls at last are you
the sleeping or the dead?

The couple on the mantelpiece
still smile as couples can —
Look on that picture and on this
and tell me who I am.

The Punch Family

"I was much affected by the internal troubles of the Punch family. I thought that with a little more tact on the part of Mrs Punch and some restraint held over a temper, naturally violent, by Mr Punch, a great deal of this sad misunderstanding might have been prevented"

(*Edmund Gosse,* Father and Son)

He was always alone in this:
each holiday, with seaside friends
who weren't his friends, he gazed
at a high tent's awful hole
and shuddered. Something amiss,
unnameable, a huge stick
pummelling his shapeless soul
like pastry. Even the jolly stripes
reminded him of blood. Amazed,
not as a child is by some party trick,
he learned from squeaking archetypes
the terror on which life depends.

And later, back at the grim hotel
which never let him out of sight
but set a righteous face against the sea
in red-bricked anger, echoes
put on flesh; "Your mother isn't well ...
this place ... the air ..." His father's voice
was hard like making deals. "She chose
to rest a little on her own this afternoon.
I had a word with them. They sent up tea.
I don't know why we come here. It's *her* choice."
Something was still unnameable but soon
that show, too, finished for the night.

At breakfast, nothing made sense.
Once more the same pain
shuddered across the table as they thrust
their glumness at each other. Why?

What huge stick in the silence
hung above them? When would it hammer down
and end this? When would she cry
or he be gone forever?
                    So, each holiday
each morning, always, one small boy must
leave them alone in this, a fixed frown
souring his heart, and, friendless, go and play
with friends, and in the evening come again.

The Boy Guru

Scene: a delicatessen
in Luton. Cast: solo.
It's the ghost of the Boy Guru's
poster again

outfacing price
reductions, taped to the window —
Green peppers, garlic, no
parmesan today, and *Peace! Peace!*

Not the moon but
cream floating on coffee;
an affluent simile
for a sect

made in our image.
Features of foie gras
(all faith is grass),
we guess at his age —

fourteen? Already
round his head
the blue has faded.
Somewhere in the sky

beyond sight
a throb of engines —
He has taken our sins;
he's flown out.

The Fair

"Welcome" they say

"By kind permission of the mayor
your town will wake tonight"

Our quoits fall short.
We choke a duck
with ping-pong balls.

Behind each dodgem's
painted snarl, a father
steering recklessly, one-handed,
as he hugs his son.

A pair of dark arms
lock at midnight, reaching
for the height from which we fell.

The corporation flower-bed
is a bearded lady.

Laws are passed.

Disco

It happens darkly
in a strange room —
"Try me" says the T-shirt
rolled to her neck.

A galaxy of little breasts
is shining with love;
the world's in a flat spin,
faster, faster.

Who cares? He does
and she does. Both.
"Turn up that music.
Play to us only!"

Clutching each other
for the light's sake
then loved once over
at its dark edge

is nothing new
and is better than nothing —
"Try me" says death
"It was always like this."

The Precinct

The precinct's new recorderie displays
Slouching torsos wired to the latest craze.

Gob-stopper lollipops and flavoured gum —
Slack mouths in motion. Let the climax come.

Albums filed like evidence of crime.
The children of the free are doing time

As time, of course, is doing them although
Only a fool would dare to tell them so.

"Man is in love and loves what vanishes" —
"Hey, baby, cool it!" Lieutenant Kojak says

"What vanishes? What vanishes is dross.
Don't give me that. Wise up and cut your loss."

His shaved head bulges on a record sleeve.
Lord, I believe; help thou mine unbelief.

A klaxon shrieks its warning down the street
"I am the maker you've prepared to meet.

The station waits for all of you. The stars
Twinkle like cookies through thick iron bars."

The discs are spun, the pick-ups disengage,
The decks are cleared. Not Heaven in a rage

But Nowhere, Never. Life's out in the cold.
The children of the free grow up, grow old.

READING HABITS

1
Installed for magazines
at Smith & Son,
"I don't know about books"
she says. She says
"In *there*. Ask Books.
We don't sell cigarettes."

2
Choosing Outsize Fiction
hugely printed —
"No!" her daughter hisses,
breaking regulations,
"No, not Bournemouth this year —
No! I can't, I can't, I can't!"

3
Behind the sliding glass
with Haig and Tio Pepe,
The Ascent of Man,
My Life, My Loves, —
A few choice titles
lean upon each other.

4
Washed in the pure Idea
but hurt by people —
Peter Wimsey, Hercule Poirot,
Ovaltine and two warm whiskies ...
Style! A clear solution,
nobody's address.

5

Each black page of the album
heaped with children — only
one of her, alone and distant
on a high cliff, reading
"I've forgotten what it was.
I once liked Mary Webb."

6

Searching the thin-sliced shelves
of little reputations
for his latest volume —
maybe Dunn will notice it this time —
"There are only 250 readers of poetry
and I know half of them."

7

This being out of Town
or almost Country, hedgehogs die
and small birds tangle with our progress
but we know their names —
The bookshops here sell Richard Jefferies,
dreams of Arcadia at dusk.

8

Commitment and anxiety
collide on Parents Evening —
"How can I make him read a book?
Is *Beano* bad for his English?"
"Are there books in your house, Mr Jones?"
"It's my wife who does the reading."

9
He likes to read at night.
She doesn't. Recently
he bought a little bedside
Anglepoise but sometimes
if she stays awake
they make love between chapters.

10
Locked behind a grille
at *Foyles for Books,* she says
"Ask him" who says
"You'll find it on the Second Floor
etc." If not,
a man outside sells chestnuts piping hot.

Party Political Broadcast

A forehead shines above its eyes
above a mouth — "These are the facts ..." —
gasping, bubbles at 9pm.

"Just so. I'm glad you asked me. Quite."
They burst, each of them, as they rise
becoming air. Our faces crowd at the rim.

Life behind glass exacts a price —
"I want to speak to you tonight ..."
The fish-tank pickles its brains.

Our democratic cat has eaten
every fish. He sits there purring
after close-down, and his smile remains.

Notes for a Talking Head

Introduced. Stand.
Thank variously. Acknowledge
applause if any.
If none make joke get laugh
however (Topical?
Local ref? Vicar? Rush-hour
if heavy indust.?)
Adjust mic. if mic./
"Can you hear at back?"
if village hall etc.
"That better?"
Begin.

Quote hand-out
"Everything in my power will be done
by the party I represent
to represent you in everything
the party has done."

This obvious.
Needless to say
time is now. Only
coward running looks behind.
Are on the move.
Past must take care of self.
Personal note: don't own
own house. Know to be others
in own position (pause)
or worse (long pause)
Quote hand-out
"None shall go empty."
Be seeing to that as far
as can as in me lies
to change the course of things.
Prices high as beanstalk.
Am no giant-killer but try.
This little/important/spot/area
forever England where I
speak to you today
of years to come and many
on the bright side too.
Remember your voice always
my voice. Never too busy etc.
People my business.
As for threatened motorway
and education have myself
car and three plus new arrival
children. Deplore as much as you do.

End. Sit.
Fumble a bit
with papers etc.
Pour glass of water.
Pour glass of water for chairman
if lady. If any
applaud other speakers.
Keep smiling.

PROFILES

1

We've found he has a concentration
problem motivating
major headache situation

problems of relating
to his headache situation
situations though the problem

with our problem is a
language situation problem and our
language is a problem situation

we do not relate to
since we never call a headache headache
though we understand.

2

We think he doubts the relevance of learning
to his home environment and
recommend a project called *The Relevance*

of Home. The relevance of school
may then be structured hopefully
in terms of individual need

by stages monitored each week and
scanned according to the pilot programme
currently ongoing at the local

Centre. We must not lose hope
or think him better off at home.
It's a question of meaningful structures.

FOUR RIDDLES
(for Oliver Burford-Mason)

1

Slickster, little vehicle, my need
is urgent as my grille of teeth.
First in the race called after me,
I fix myself a paradise of stench.
From groomed saloons, sleek
as my body and engaged on
larger dirty business, gangsters
know each other by my name.

2

Who knows me? The dry leaves
frisk to my bagatelles; they whisper
snatch by snatch my darker meaning.
Twigs that scrape your bedroom window
behind curtains, tracing
fear on glass, and dismal clouds
that lunge across the moon
are mine. Who knows me?

3

If I am up, the children's eyes
are dancing and their shadows
blackly agitate the patterned wall.
Midway, my comfortable glow
delights in brass and mellows furniture.
If I am down, forgotten beauties
nod beside me, picturing
the blaze of passion when we leaped together.

4

My fate, alas, is inescapable.
No sweet princess will turn me back
to this, nor (I suppose)
would anybody want to — save, perhaps,
a kid with jam-jars doing
Nature Study. Oh, the tedium
of waiting in this muddy water
for my resurrection when I croak.

Mr Cartwright's Counting Rhyme

One, two
You, boy, yes I'm talking to you

three, four
I've wiped the floor

five, six
with others of your kind. Your tricks

seven, eight
come centuries too late

nine, ten
for experienced men

eleven, twelve
like myself

thirteen, fourteen
so just be careful to be more seen

fifteen, sixteen
than heard, or preferably not seen

seventeen, eighteen
at all. Or you could stop baiting

nineteen, twenty
and pity me.

Buttercups
(for Hannah Chambers)

A golden boat comes sailing in,
Buttercups heaped from deck to brim
And all for a proud Babylonian king.

But Nebuchadnezzar's grizzly chin
Is thick with whiskers, the daft old thing.
What use are buttercups to him?

Pantomime Cat

Black cat, Puss,
how you sadden us
with your ancient fur,
all that dust on the air
when you beat your breast —
Oh rest, rest
in the peace you deserve
for having served
to delight us all
so we still recall
a little of how
our kids love you now
who cannot see
how inevitably
your huge, lidded eyes
hold no surprise,
how your whiskers are split,
your grin is a slit,
your tail hangs down,
how your high renown
has shrunk to a dream,
hot-dogs and ice-cream,
and your dull boots tread
on the dead, on the dead.

Paterfamilias

A ravished bride and her abundant progeny
Sit round the table, mirrored in mahogany.

Which of the children have their father's face?
The eldest son performs a Latin grace.

Enter Jessie from the Servants' Quarters.
Marcus is in love with both her daughters.

Cecil's ambitious; his amours are Gallic.
Ralph finds the pepper-pot distinctly phallic.

Jessie brings a dish and lifts its lid;
Monica has told her what Hugh did

But she herself has always fancied John —
One needs the sweetmeats when one's tooth is long.

Gertrude is senior on the distaff side;
She's been an angel since her father died.

Sarah reads novels; such a pity she
Cannot make sense of sensibility.

Annette likes stories from the underworld;
Inside those velvet shoes her toes are curled.

Which leaves plain Jane, her mother's greatest joy
Despite some trouble with the gardener's boy.

The portrait on the blue-veined mantelpiece
Of course is Father, prior to his decease.

A pair of urns, Victorian-Hellenic
(Ralph declares that they're distinctly phallic)

Flank the gilded frame on either hand.
Ralph was the son he tried to understand.

His ideal was Arcadian — a chaste
Unravished bride of quietness and taste

Depicted palely on a brittle surface.
Searching in every child of his for her face

He found, alas, another and another
Resolute facsimile of its mother.

Now they sit, without him, round the table
Fleshing out a Great Victorian Fable,

Demonstrating sadly how it feels
To be the sediment of High Ideals,

An odd, bewildered human residue —
Five boys: John, Marcus, Cecil, Ralph and Hugh,

Their sisters and their mother. What a life!
So much depends on choosing the right wife.

A Proper Caution

When Grandpa on my mother's side,
The playful one, rolled up his sleeves
And tap-danced at the carpet's edge
At tea-time, as he often did,
His second wife was not amused —
"How strangely Arthur still behaves!"
Embarrassed by his flashing shoes,
She frowned as if she'd signed the pledge.

So when a vagueness called The Arts
Became the thing for me to do
And not my father's father's firm
Which claimed my father, it was said
"Poor Arthur's silly fits and starts
Are coming out in John." They knew
Exactly where I'd got it from —
"To put such ideas in his head!"

But what they never knew was this —
The time when, at his study desk,
He showed me with such seriousness
How business letters should be brisk
And always end Yours Faithfully
Then smiled, as from the living-room
Came "Arthur! Don't you want your tea? ..."

He didn't dance that afternoon.

The Wordsworth Concordance

Less than two hundred references to *Child.*
Innocence, surprisingly, rates ninety-three.
Was he not what we thought he was? Compiled
At length at Cornell University
It should be accurate enough, yet *Birth*
Still gets a meagre eighty-seven's worth.

Try *Death.* A hundred and ninety various deaths —
Mere marginal improvement there. And *Dead?*
Not often. The Romantic shibboleths
Disport themselves most dismally. Instead,
We might as well spend no more wasteful time,
Settling for *Nothing* with its ninety-nine.

But what's this list, five solid pages long?
Yes, yes. Of course. The complement to *Dove,*
Where heaven is, than whom more truly strong?,
Etcetera, etcetera. O LOVE,
You clear a clean eight hundred, give or take,
And Poetry's back in business, no mistake!

Paperweight

Exact, at the desk's
centre, a small globe
squats on completion.
Life has arranged itself
just so; his world
is somehow in order.

Nothing. No snowscape
shivers its flakes.
Each night, in a warm room,
he's always happy —
What treacherous glass
has shown him this?

"You" it says "are the
Middle-aged Old
Master. Read the reviews —
I am pure crystal,
a safe weight on your papers
forever. Trust me."

Nothing. Outside,
the snow quickens endeavour
elsewhere. Here is only
the reflection of peace
like a white sheet endlessly
becoming ice.

Exact, at his mind's
centre, a cold globe
squats on contentment.
Call it fame, a lifetime
trapped in amber,
the world at his feet.

The Stuffed Goldfinch

I have no business
on this golden bough
which prose
would call branch anyway.

But a golden branch
suggests only
brochures of the Hartford
Insurance Co.

That won't do —
Life was a parapluie.
I looked at blackbirds
in thirteen ways.

Now, without rain
or sun, I turn
in all directions
imagining weather.

Joseph Conrad on TV

Says the accomplished
actor, so resembling
those profiles, those intense
sharp-bearded portraits
with the famous
lonely eyes, "As you
might feel your lungs,
your heart, your liver,
I could *feel* my brain, yes,
often when I wrote
it was my brain I felt
but could not hold it."

Conrad on *Omnibus*
to tell the world
what Shaw once said
so unforgettably
"Your books won't do!"
A spotlit maestro, brilliant
in studio gloom, he
chain-smokes, brushing ash
urbanely from a period suit
and still insisting
"I could feel my brain,
it was my brain
I felt" as if such words
might cut the lights
and end it, end it.

The Big Director

He's tired now, always —
Eighteen legendary stone of
failure, heaped on a canvas chair.
He blames the studio.

Art, of course, of a kind,
is what he's after — the capital A,
the class product —
but this, too, is a B feature:

so he sleeps on the lot,
so what the hell anyway? —
let it go out, this dumb show
from the place of skulls.

And if he wakes it's to say
"Do me a love scene, boobies" —
to walk off, to call his wife,
to come back yawning.

Emily Dickinson Was Right About This

"Art" she wrote "is a house
Which tries to be haunted"
Always the same choice —
Wake the dead
Or pack up and go.
Art is Yes or No.

Even after a lifetime
To move out, admit
"The place was fine,
I liked it
But who came there?"
Staying is nowhere.

Yet all of us stay
Or, at least, most.
Who dares say
He has seen no ghost
And never will?
Truth can kill.

Safer, by far, to wait
In a pleasant room,
Plan, decorate —
It must happen soon.
Get off to a good start.
Patience is an art.

BETHLEHEM 1861
(Men's ward)

1
The Word in black
administers to
Garrick poses
struck forever.

2
Is that a dagger?
It's called
sunlight and
it cuts each throat.

3
Porcelain skulls.
Absences
affixed to torsos
not their own.

4
Such eyes!
The coinage of reason
spun in them
and lost.

5
Close the artist's
album, draw
thick curtains
round this muttering.

6
The Word in black
is speechless,
leaves beside each bed
an empty chair.

SISTERS

1
There's a smile at the door.
I have not said Come In.
It pauses.

It has not
asked to come in. Its pause
precedes it.

This is how always
it announces itself
in silence.

We are amused by each other.
Sometimes I think
it likes me.

Why else come again?
What possible
intention?

Smile, I like you too.
You *know*. You never
say Cheer Up.

Today, if I can,
I shall let you in.
Be patient.

Wait! Don't go!
I'm arranging my face
to meet you.

2
There's a tear at the window.
I'm prepared for this.
It looks in.

Such a moist gaze
is so persuasive, almost
eye to eye.

A tiny globe
of distant landscapes.
Open view.

We meet like this.
We share a treacherous knowledge
in our dreams.

Outside, the dark
around one precious gem
is settling.

Tear, the proper address
for tears is
Thee and Thou —

a watery poetic,
glass between us, glittering
sentiment.

Stay there! My life
is locked in your perfection
endlessly.

3

There's a kiss at the bedside.
I know how it entered.
A warm breeze.

I was always looking
elsewhere before. It
knows the odds.

But not this time:
the others have warned me,
gentle pair.

The room enlarges.
Love comes quietly from
its corners.

What surprise!
The cautious touch, my
readiness.

Kiss, you seal everything.
The sibilance of
parted lips.

You are first and last.
Between two darknesses you
spin the thread.

Frail measurement of light,
I am your centre,
This is it.

Off the Hook

So many hands reach out for them
and leave them standing;
office telephones — "Hello?" ...
A new girl paints her nails.

They bark at their reflections
in the cold formica —
"Hello. Hello. Hello ..."
To each its empty cradle.

Someone has gone for someone
everywhere. Ubiquitous glass
dispenses sunlight to a vacancy
of table-tops and chairs.

Alas, the tiny voices!
These are the lost, the hopeful,
trapped in a mouthpiece
waiting to be put through.

One by one, they die
at the end of patience —
a perspective of upturned turtles
on Christmas Island.

Six o'clock encroaches
and the tide is roaring.
No one will come now.
Even the sun goes home.

The Bay

The bay opens its arms to yachts
for Summer. Watching them
can take the edge off distance.

Nothing is now too far, and not
too close. The world's gaze rests
at last on mild horizons.

This is the lovely seaside, cleansing.
All goes out to the yachts
on warm air, including our hearts,
and leaves the children in a rock-pool
with flotillas of newsprint.
Water-logged, their day goes under.

Colour Supplement

Today, a feature on The Great Depression —
Swing bands orchestrate the *Sunday Times*.

A crooner pins a rose to his lapel;
its blush illuminates a hired tuxedo.

You, the night, the music and our future.
Monstrous lustres glittering with hope ...

We take the floor. A world of spectral dancers
brush against your costly dress like leaves

and leaves come tumbling now around us;
little blood-clots thicken in the air.

What can we do? Who pays the bitter piper
must be paid for, but the *Sunday Times*

still makes it seem enough like history, safe
and distant, as the dancers cling together

sleeping on their feet, and as the lights
go down on England, softly, one by one.

AT PRESERVATION HALL

1
A hat comes round:
this is their last number.

For fifty cents
the Saints will march us home —

Those grizzled heads,
those baggy trousers,

shoes in a stomping row
of toe-caps shining.

2
Wound up, the horns
nestle in velvet,

each to its black box
snapped tight, homeward ...

Silent curvatures
whose rest is a golden echo:

bones, bones,
them dry bones disassembled.

The Pattern

Three ships: the pattern's incomplete.
To give it meaning we imagine water.

For truth's sake, a dangerous ocean
cold and dark beneath the pretty frieze.

What warmth there is acknowledges
that love survives by such arrangement —

Happy Christmas. Precious words.
To give them meaning we imagine God.

AT SAINT-REMY

1
The sun applies
its terrible strict shadows
and your face amongst them
hurting mine.

2
Such heat is locked
within my colours
bringing even stone
to parturition.

3
Each natural gap
reveals its creature,
crusted pigments
for the connoisseur.

4
Into the dark,
a rim of candles
leaping with light
towards extinction.

5
Elemental skies,
rapacious sunflowers
and my face pressed closer
hurting yours.

Table Talk

The wood's high polish smeared their faces —
featureless as stocking-masks or
she said like the birth of kittens.

So they dwelt on their reflections
but could not agree. Alarmed, his fingers
searched out objects and her hands

avoided touch. O guilty world
where kittens frisk in stocking-masks ...
A meal lay finished on the table

and the evidence seemed fixed forever
in those lip-prints and that
patterned saucer slagged with ash.

Looking Like Rain

A sullen darkening around our faces
holds us apart. Once more, the world
moves in on itself and it looks like rain.

After, there are no words for what rain looked like;
only for how, with a new brightness,
the air heals behind what has passed through.